Words of Encouragement

Copyright © 1980 Lion Publishing

Published by
Lion Publishing plc
Sandy Lane West, Oxford, England
ISBN 0 7459 1973 1 (paperback)
ISBN 0 7459 2107 8 (cased)
Albatross Books Pty Ltd
PO Box 320, Sutherland, NSW 2232, Australia
ISBN 0 7324 0254 9 (paperback)
ISBN 0 7324 0464 9 (cased)

First edition in this format 1991

Photographs by Patricia and Charles Aithie - ffotograff.

Quotations from *Good News Bible*, copyright 1966, 1971 and 1976 American
Bible Society; published by the Bible Societies and Collins.

Printed and bound in Singapore

◆ *Words of* ◆
ENCOURAGEMENT

A LION BOOK
Oxford · Batavia · Sydney

◆ I WILL SAVE ◆

God says, 'I will save those who love me
    and will protect those who know me as Lord.
When they call to me, I will answer them;
    when they are in trouble, I will be with them.
    I will rescue them and honour them.
I will reward them with long life;
    I will save them.'

PSALM 91:14–16

◆ GOD, THE SOURCE OF ◆ ENCOURAGEMENT

Everything written in the Scriptures was written to teach us, in order that we might have hope through the patience and encouragement which the Scriptures give us. And may God, the source of patience and encouragement, enable you to have the same point of view among yourselves by following the example of Christ Jesus, so that all of you together may praise with one voice the God and Father of our Lord Jesus Christ.

ROMANS 15:4–6

◆ THE FATHER'S CARE ◆

For only a penny you can buy two sparrows, yet not one sparrow falls to the ground without your Father's consent. As for you, even the hairs of your head have all been counted. So do not be afraid; you are worth much more than many sparrows!

MATTHEW 10:29–31

◆ DON'T BE DISCOURAGED ◆

Let us rid ourselves of everything that gets in the way, and of the sin which holds on to us so tightly, and let us run with determination the race that lies before us. Let us keep our eyes fixed on Jesus, on whom our faith depends from beginning to end. He did not give up because of the cross! On the contrary, because of the joy that was waiting for him, he thought nothing of the disgrace of dying on the cross, and he is now seated at the right-hand side of God's throne.

Think of what he went through; how he put up with so much hatred from sinners! So do not let yourselves become discouraged and give up.

HEBREWS 12:1–3

◆ JOY AND GLADNESS ◆

Even though the fig-trees have no fruit and no grapes
    grow on the vines,
even though the olive-crop fails and the fields produce
    no corn,
even though the sheep all die and the cattle-stalls are
    empty,
I will still be joyful and glad, because the Lord God is
    my saviour.
The Lord gives me strength.
    He makes me sure-footed as a deer, and keeps me
    safe on the mountains.

HABAKKUK 3:17–19

✦ GOD WITH US ✦

The Lord himself will lead you and be with you. He will not fail you or abandon you, so do not lose courage or be afraid.

DEUTERONOMY 31:8

✦ GOD'S LOVE IS SO GREAT ✦

The Lord is merciful and loving,
  slow to become angry and full of constant love.
He does not keep on rebuking; he is not angry for ever.
He does not punish us as we deserve or repay us for
  our sins and wrongs.
As high as the sky is above the earth,
  so great is his love for those who honour him.
As far as the east is from the west,
  so far does he remove our sins from us.
As kind as a father is to his children,
  so kind is the Lord to those who honour him.

PSALM 103:8–13

✦ YOUR REWARD ✦

Whatever you do, work at it with all your heart, as though you were working for the Lord and not for men. Remember that the Lord will give you as a reward what he has kept for his people. For Christ is the real Master you serve.

COLOSSIANS 3:23–24

◆ A PLACE FOR YOU ◆

'Do not be worried and upset,' Jesus told them. 'Believe in God and believe also in me. There are many rooms in my Father's house, and I am going to prepare a place for you. I would not tell you this if it were not so. And after I go and prepare a place for you, I will come back and take you to myself, so that you will be where I am.'

JOHN 14:1–3

◆ ENCOURAGE ONE ◆
ANOTHER

Let us come near to God with a sincere heart and a sure faith, with hearts that have been purified from a guilty conscience and with bodies washed with clean water. Let us hold on firmly to the hope we profess, because we can trust God to keep his promise. Let us be concerned for one another, to help one another to show love and to do good. Let us not give up the habit of meeting together, as some are doing. Instead, let us encourage one another all the more, since you see that the Day of the Lord is coming nearer.

HEBREWS 10:22–25

◆ AN ETERNAL PROMISE ◆

Jesus Christ is the same yesterday, today, and for ever.

HEBREWS 13:8

✦ MY PLANS FOR YOU ✦

I alone know the plans I have for you, plans to bring
you prosperity and not disaster, plans to bring about
the future you hope for. Then you will call to me. You
will come and pray to me, and I will answer you. You
will seek me, and you will find me because you will
seek me with all your heart.

JEREMIAH 29:11–13

✦ GOD'S CHILDREN ✦

For the Spirit that God has given you does not make you slaves and cause you to be afraid; instead, the Spirit makes you God's children, and by the Spirit's power we cry out to God, 'Father! my Father!' God's Spirit joins himself to our spirits to declare that we are God's children. Since we are his children, we will possess the blessings he keeps for his people, and we will also possess with Christ what God has kept for him; for if we share Christ's suffering, we will also share his glory.

ROMANS 8:15–17

◆ FREE FROM WORRY ◆

Humble yourselves, then, under God's mighty hand, so that he will lift you up in his own good time. Leave all your worries with him, because he cares for you.

1 PETER 5:6–7

◆ WHEN JESUS COMES AGAIN ◆

There will be the shout of command, the archangel's voice, the sound of God's trumpet, and the Lord himself will come down from heaven. Those who have died believing in Christ will rise to life first; then we who are living at that time will be gathered up along with them in the clouds to meet the Lord in the air. And so we will always be with the Lord. So then, encourage one another with these words.

1 THESSALONIANS 4:16–18

◆ GOD, MY GUIDE AND ◆
STRENGTH

I always stay close to you, and you hold me by the
    hand.
You guide me with your instruction and at the end you
    will receive me with honour.
What else have I in heaven but you?
    Since I have you, what else could I want on earth?
My mind and my body may grow weak,
    but God is my strength;
    he is all I ever need.

PSALM 73:23–26

◆ NEVER GIVE UP ◆

Thanks be to God who gives us the victory through our Lord Jesus Christ! So then, my dear brothers, stand firm and steady. Keep busy always in your work for the Lord, since you know that nothing you do in the Lord's service is ever useless.

Let us not become tired of doing good; for if we do not give up, the time will come when we will reap the harvest.

1 CORINTHIANS 15:57–58; GALATIANS 6:9

◆ SECURE IN GOD'S LOVE ◆

Who, then, can separate us from the love of Christ? Can trouble do it, or hardship or persecution or hunger or poverty or danger or death?...

No, in all these things we have complete victory through him who loved us! For I am certain that nothing can separate us from his love: neither death nor life, neither angels nor other heavenly rulers or powers, neither the present nor the future, neither the world above nor the world below—there is nothing in all creation that will ever be able to separate us from the love of God which is ours through Christ Jesus our Lord.

ROMANS 8:35, 38–39

✦ ANSWERED PRAYER ✦

And I tell you more: whenever two of you on earth agree about anything you pray for, it will be done for you by my Father in heaven. For where two or three come together in my name, I am there with them.

MATTHEW 18:19–20

◆ EVERY NEED MET ◆

With all his abundant wealth through Christ Jesus, my God will supply all your needs. To our God and Father be the glory for ever and ever! Amen.

PHILIPPIANS 4:19–20